AGILITY
IS FUN

A step by step guide for beginners and experienced competitors

by Ruth Hobday

**Illustrations and photographs by
Sandra Russell (Russell Fine Art).**

OUR DOGS PUB

'OUR DOGS' PUBLISHING CO. LTD.,
5 Oxford Road, Station Approach, Manchester M60 1SX

Telephone: 061 236 2660
Fax: 061 236 5534

Ruth Hobday, Willow Batch, Carding Mill Valley, Church Stretton, Shropshire. Telephone: 0694 723126.

All photographs and diagrams by Sandra Russell of RUSSELL FINE ART (and 'OUR DOGS' Staff Photographer), 33 Sycamore Road, Eccles, Greater Manchester M30 8LH. Telephone: 061 789 4819.

First published, 1989.

© **'Our Dogs' Publishing Company Limited.**

ISBN 0-903034 10 7

'Our Dogs' Publishing Company Limited

Typeset by C.T.L. Typesetting, Ring Road, West Park, Leeds, LS16 6EB.

Printed by Gibbons Barford Print, Centenary House, Wednesfield Road, Wolverhampton, WV10 0JA.

ABOUT RUTH HOBDAY

From an early age at school Ruth was involved in competitive sports — especially athletics. She had always wanted a dog but her first, a Cocker Spaniel called Rusty, didn't do very well at obedience classes!

Moving to Shropshire she then acquired a cross breed, Kim, and Sheba, a small and rather nervous Shetland Sheepdog. As Sheba kept breaking stays, Ruth turned to Kim, the cross breed, who in 1970-71 began to impress winning at Beginners & Novice classes. By 1980 Ruth with Riki, also a Sheltie, 'discovered' the world of Agility and enjoyed its more exciting atmosphere.

In 1986 Riki and Border Collie 'Kwippy' were eclipsed by 'Heidi' now so well known as the Agility Dog of the Year in 1987 and 1988.

Ruth started obedience instruction in the late 60's and instructed at Shrewsbury Dog Training Club for about fifteen years. In 1981 Shrewsbury began Agility and Ruth became their instructor, later joined by Jo Evason. She has also run her own local obedience class for the last 12 years.

Ruth has now given up her career in teaching and has become a full time Agility trainer since 1987 having built a whole new set of equipment from scratch and has been running the 'Hurricane Dog Training Centre' in Shropshire since April 1988.

WHAT PEOPLE SAY!

Visitors to the Hurricane Dog Training Centre are amazed at the progress of both dog & human! Here is a selection of recent comments:-

"If anyone had told me I would have enjoyed a whole day in the open air, with rain and no shops I wouldn't have believed it. At the end Penny had a go at everything!"

Mrs J Manley, Manchester

"Thank you for a most helpful and informative course which stood us in great stead.
The Hurricane School is a brilliant idea, we wouldn't have had a clue before attending."

Mr & Mrs Hillsden, Harrogate

"As you said, its great fun! Brook obviously enjoyed his day too."

Patricia Wallis.

"We found your training exercises and willingness to discuss things in depth most helpful."

Mr & Mrs Tappin, Oxford.

"I very much appreciated the individual and fresh advice which could only come from the depth of thought which you have given Agility. At our club we performed well above our previous efforts."

Martin Pollard, Essex.

ABOUT THE BOOK

'Agility is Fun' is written in an interesting and readable style and is profusely illustrated by photos and diagrams throughout for greater clarity and should be of use to agility enthusiasts at all levels of ability. A must for all serious agility enthusiasts throughout the world, it covers the introduction of the beginner dog to all the items of equipment and also stresses the importance of control training for all dogs. The control exercises described throughout the book should be of great benefit to both the beginner and the more advanced dog.

ACKNOWLEDGEMENTS

The author and publishers gratefully acknowledge the help and assistance of the following companies and individuals in the production of this book:-

Pedigree Petfoods for their support; Jackie Manley and Dawn McConnell of 'OUR DOGS' for production, Maurice Weldon of CTL Typesetters and not forgetting all our friends both human and four legged who appear in the photographs.

CONTENTS

Chapter	Page

1. Introduction 3

2. A Dog For Agility.
     — The dog you have or a new pup 4
     — Choosing a pup for agility - breed - size - sex 7
     — Before going to select a pup 12

3. Early Puppy Training.
     — House training 15
     — Teaching the pup his name 15
     — Getting used to the lead 15
     — Coming when called 15

4. Getting & Keeping Your Dog Fit for Agility.
     — Roadwork 17
     — Warming up (before training or competition) 17
     — The age to start agility 18

5. Early Control Training.
     — Heelwork 19
     — Instant down 20
     — Wait on command 21
     — Recall 22
     — Send away 22
     — On the Agility Course 23

6. Ready for Agility Training.
     — Clubs 25
     — Equipment for dog & handler 25
     — Commands 28
     — Praise & play 30

7. Teaching The Dog To Jump 31

8. Teaching the Contact Obstacles.
     — Scale or 'A' frame 35
     — Dog walk 38
     — Cross over or dog cross 41
     — See-saw 42

9. Weaving Poles 49

10. Other Obstacles.
— Pause box 57
— Table 59
— Tunnel 62
— Tyre 67
— Long Jump 70

11. Different Types of Jumps.
— Parallel planks 75
— Gate 75
— Brush 76
— Wall 76
— Single pole 77
— Spread 78
— Water Jump 79
— Well 80

12. Jumping Exercises & Control Training 83

13. Conclusion 111

Heidi (Sealight Hurricane), to whom this book is dedicated.

Val Mackay who started it all.

INTRODUCTION

It was my friend Val Mackay who started it all. Telling her about the articles I had been asked to write for **'OUR DOGS'**, she suddenly said, "I should make sure you keep the copyright so that you can use them in a book one day." Write a book — me? Well, I began to think.

I'd always been very conscious of how easy it was to play around at an agility training session, without really training your dog. For a long time I'd kept a note-book in which I wrote down my dog's exercises, so that I didn't waste time. Perhaps other people would be interested in my methods of training. Anyway, it would be very useful for me to have all my exercises worked out for when I began running my agility training courses.

I mentioned the idea to Vincent Hogan the Managing Director of **'OUR DOGS'** and he was very interested. After I had finished teaching, I had three months free before I began my business, I set to work.

I decided that several small books would be better than one large one, for two reasons: Firstly, taking it a book at a time made it seem a lot less daunting a task, and secondly, this way we could keep the price down. And so Book One was written.

I have really enjoyed writing it, although it took longer than I expected.

The methods described are ones that I have used and found successful, but I've learnt that every dog you train needs different handling. What works with one, may not work with another. I learn something new with every dog or handler I train — so if your method is different, but successful, stick to it. If not, then don't be afraid to try something else.

I'd like to thank Val MacKay for the original idea and for reading the manuscript through for me. Jo Evason for checking all the exercises to see if they were understandable. John and Jane Coleman on whose land I have my agility course and without whose help I could never have realised the dream of setting up my own business. Jackie Manley for typing the manuscript and, the members of Shrewsbury, Newton Heath and Chadkirk agility groups for their help with photographs.

I hope everyone who buys the book will enjoy it and hopefully find it useful.

Ruth Hobday

1. A DOG FOR AGILITY

Most people who decide they want to have a go at agility already own a dog. It may just be a pet or they may do Obedience, Working Trials or Breed showing with it. The first thing you have to decide is whether the dog you have is suitable or should you get a pup especially for agility.

Virtually any dog, so long as it is fit, can do and enjoy agility.

I would advise you to have a go with the dog you have if at all possible.

Then, later, decide whether to buy a pup specifically for agility.

If you do decide to get a pup, remember that it will be at least 12 months before you can really start agility training. No dog under 12 months old, is allowed to compete in agility. No serious agility training should be started until the pup's bones have matured, which can be as late as 15 to 18 months for large breeds.

Many breeds that people do not normally expect to work love agility, like the Dalmatian or Gordon Setter.

The new agility handler is bound to make mistakes to begin with — indeed, you learn by your mistakes — but it is better to learn with a mature dog than a youngster.

Before you begin agility training you should be sure that the dog has no physical disability, such as hip displasia, and is not overweight. It is not fair to jump a fat dog. If he is overweight, diet him first. If you have any doubt as to the physical fitness of your dog, I advise you to check with a vet before beginning training.

Choosing a pup, for agility.

If you do decide to get a pup, there are several things to consider.

Many successful club teams contain a variety of different breeds. Dundee Club Team won at Crufts in 1988 and '87.

2nd in the Crufts Team event 1988 was another mixed breed team representing Woodside Club.

Breed. There are many different breeds doing agility very successfully. You don't have to have a Collie or a G.S.D., although they are ideal breeds for the sport.

G.S.D's seldom seem to move as fast as the Border Collies, but are popular because of their steady reliability.

Many people say agility is becoming a Collie sport as so many Collies win prizes, but they forget that there are a lot more Collies in the sport than any other breed.

I'm not saying don't get a Collie, but don't think that by getting one you are bound to win. There are lots of Collies who may never win.

I have two Border Collies. They have been trained in the same way and they can both run as fast as each other — let out of my gate for a run, they race off neck and neck. However on an agility course, they are totally different. Kwippy does everything, but never seems to be really happy. Although she gets an occasional place, she will never be a big winner. Heidi, on the other hand, loves agility, can never do too much and gives it everything she's got. On an agility course there's nothing else on her mind but getting as fast as possible from one obstacle to another. I'm sure this love of agility is born in a dog and this is what makes the difference within the breed.

Border Collies are probably the most popular dogs used for agility.

Apart from Collies and G.S.D's, what other breeds are successfully competing?

Golden Retrievers. There are several good Golden Retrievers doing agility, some of which are very fast. Barrie Harvey's 'Charles Harvest Sun' ran at Olympia 1987, the first Goldie to qualify.

Belgian Shepherd Dogs. A couple of years ago there seemed to be nearly as many Tervuerens as G.S.D's in agility. There are fewer now, but still they are a very successful breed.

B.S.D's of the three main varieties can be seen competing in agility.

Boxers. Although not as fast as the Collies, the Boxer is an excellent, and usually very reliable, jumper.

Labradors. Again, perhaps not so fast, but very successful at times.

Shelties. Not very popular for agility at the moment, but a favourite of mine as Riki my Sheltie, got me going in agility and, was the first (and so far only Sheltie) to run at Olympia.

Riki was a large Sheltie and not really fast enough, but I am sure that a normal sized Sheltie (under 15″), running in mini classes could be a great success.

Poodles.
All three sizes of Poodle compete successfully, usually being very good jumpers.

These are just a few breeds — there are many more, plus of course, some excellent cross-breeds, so don't feel restricted when choosing a pup for agility.

Size. With the increase in popularity of mini classes, having a small dog is no problem.

One of the many Mini dogs currently competing in Agility.

Most of the smaller breeds like the Lancashire Heeler and the Yorkie, enjoy agility.

However, a very large dog — e.g.
Great Dane or St Bernard, is not really suitable for agility.

Adorable as many puppies are, their adult build may not really be suited for agility (eg the St Bernard or Tibetan Mastiff).

These dogs would have difficulty getting through the tyre and, would need to go down on their knees to get through most tunnels. Also the width of dog walk and see-saw planks may be rather narrow for very large dogs. Perhaps we need maxi agility as well as mini.

Sex. Selection of dog or bitch. This is really a personal choice. Bitches may be slightly easier to train than dogs, who often have other things on their minds. Really either sex is just as good for agility. Some large G.S.D. dogs may be slightly heavy and, not as fast as the bitches of that breed.

Going to Select a Pup

Even before you go to see a litter of pups, you should do your homework and find out all you can about the parents and their particular line. Check on hip scores and determine whether both parents have passed eye tests if applicable for that breed. An agility dog must be sound and, able to see. A lot of heartbreak can be saved by thorough investigation beforehand. Of course you can be extremely unlucky and still get a pup with some inherited defect, but this is more unlikely from tested parents.

When you have decided on the litter you are going to get a pup from, try to go and see them a week or two before they are ready to leave. Take time to watch them all at play. See which are the extroverts (usually better at agility). Clap your hands or drop your keys and see how the pups react — this also checks that there is no hearing problem.

Try to meet both parents when selecting a puppy so that you can assess their temperament and find out as much as you can about their particular line.

If you are not happy with the litter, don't be persuaded to take one. It is much better to take your time over the selection of a pup, than to regret it later.

As soon as you get your puppy home his training begins.

2. EARLY PUPPY TRAINING

House Training

I'm not going to say much about this — it is well covered in many dog training books. Care and sympathetic handling when house training a pup are very important, as it is the start of the relationship you build up with your dog.

Teaching the Pup His Name

A really good agility dog responds instantly to his name and, training for this should be started immediately. Use the pup's name a lot and praise lavishly when he responds.

Play is vital, and time spent playing with a puppy will pay great dividends later. Use the name often when playing, so that the pup learns to associate his name with a pleasant experience.

If you call the pup's name and get no response, take some action. Clap your hands or make a noise of some sort until you do get a response, then use the name again and make a big fuss of the pup.

Getting The Pup Used to The Lead

As soon as the pup has settled into his new home, you should first get him used to wearing a light collar (not a check chain), then to having a light lead attached.

At first just let the pup drag the lead around, watching him to see it doesn't get caught anywhere. When he's used to this, catch hold of the end of the lead and call the pup, at the same time gently jerking the lead. Call him to you and give lots of praise and, play with him. Repeat this several times each session.

Taught in this way the pup won't resent the lead and you'll be ready when its time to start heelwork.

Coming When Called

This is very important for any dog and, essential for an agility dog. On an agility course the dog must come the instant it is called — there is no time to think about it. Your aim is to teach the pup that he must always come when called. The trick in doing this, is never to call a young pup unless you are almost certain he will come. Don't call him if he's half-way down a rabbit hole or tearing off to talk to his best pal. If you do call him and he doesn't come, you are teaching him that he doesn't always have to. Instead call the pup when you are sure he will come.

Prepare his food while he's in the garden; then go out, dish in hand and call him. When you're out and you see the pup rushing towards you, stoop down and call him. Give lots of praise when he gets to you. OK he was coming anyway, but if you do this often enough he will get to associate 'come' with a really enjoyable experience and hopefully, will always come when called.

If you take the pup out on a long line (about 30 feet), you have a way to enforce the command. Now you can occasionally call him from an interesting scent etc. Call him, if he doesn't come immediately take action — a jerk on the line and repeat the command. Make him come, then give lots and lots of praise. Be fair to the pup, don't do this too often. Two or three times with instant and enthusiastic praise, will have a lot more effect than a lot of nagging.

Take every opportunity to call the pup when you're sure he'll come and, keep it fun — call him, praise and play, then release him. Don't let the pup associate being called and put on the lead with the end of fun and freedom. When out with the pup running free, call him and put the lead on, praise and play with him, do a little heelwork, then have a game and let him go again. Repeat this several times each session and he'll soon enjoy coming to have his lead on.

If you teach the pup this way, you will eventually train him to always come when called. The most important thing is not to call when you are not sure he'll come. I know this is difficult and, there will be times when you feel you must try and call him. I've got over this problem by teaching a whistle command as well.

When I'm out with a young pup and I need to call him, but I'm unsure he'll come immediately, I whistle instead. As soon as I've got his attention and he starts to come, then I use his name and the 'come' command. By using a whistle you still have a way to call the dog, but name and 'come' must always mean instant obedience.

3. GETTING YOUR DOG FIT
FOR AGILITY

If you decide to start agility training with an older dog, who up to now has only been a pet, and may be slightly overweight, you must think about getting him fit first.

Roadwork

I find the best way to get a dog really fit is by doing roadwork. Not just taking your dog for a walk on the road, but fast roadwork — the dog must break into a trot. I jog about 2 miles on the road every day with my dogs, and they are very fit — it helps me too.

I first began this roadwork after Riki, my Sheltie, injured a muscle in his leg. Starting very gradually and increasing the distance daily, I soon got him fit again. He seemed to go better than ever, so I've kept it up since. Doing this type of roadwork you have to keep the dog on the lead, so that you can keep up a steady pace.

Once you start agility training and the dog is jumping low jumps, you can work on building up the jumping muscles before asking the dog to jump full height.

Put 2 or 3 small jumps (1' maximum) in a row or a circle and, run the dog over them several times a day. A 2' long jump could be included. Early control training can be incorporated into this exercise which, should ensure your dog is fit before doing any big obstacles. A dog whose muscles are soft is much more likely to injure himself, if he mistimes a jump or, slips on a contact obstacle, than a really fit dog.

Warming up Before Training or Competition

No athlete would think of jumping or sprinting without a good warm up first. The same should apply to dog agility. However, you don't need to jump a dog to warm him up. I don't believe practice jumps at a show are a good thing, because they are often misused.

I find the best way to warm dog and handler up, is to do fast heelwork incorporating lots of turns. This can be done in and around the agility obstacles, which in itself is very good training, or can be done right away from the agility area.

Age to Start Agility Training

Kennel Club rules state that puppies under 12 calendar months of age are not eligible for competition in Agility Tests. Although this refers to competition, it is a good rule to apply to training also. This gives the dog's bones time to mature, before you ask him to jump and land repeatedly or, risk him jumping off obstacles, e.g. the top of the dog walk.

With big, heavy breeds, it is best to wait until 15 or even 18 months old before beginning obstacle and jump training.

Naturally most people with a young pup are keen to get started. A lot of essential control training can be done with a youngster, so that as soon as he is old enough for real agility training, there will be no hold ups because the handler lacks control.

Unlike the dogs, handlers can start from a very early age!

4. EARLY CONTROL TRAINING

To do any good in agility classes, the handler must be able to control the dog by voice and signals alone. A lot of basic control training can be done before the dog is old enough to begin jumping. Even with an older dog, time spent on control training will pay dividends when competing. Often it is the ability to stop the dog from taking the wrong obstacle that wins the class. Many judges put a trap or two in their courses, and the dog that responds instantly to the handler, has a distinct advantage.

What sort of control training should you do? The following are all excellent exercises to do with a young pup, or an older dog, that will help in later agility training.

Heelwork

This is often needed in competition to get from one obstacle to another through tricky parts of the course.

Once the young pup is happy with a collar and lead, begin with very short stretches of fast heelwork, trying to keep the pup's attention all the time. Have a toy in your hand and after a few steps, play with the pup before going off again. Make a real game of it and keep the sessions short, so the pup never gets bored.

As the pup progresses, you can begin to add turns, teaching a different command to turn the dog each way. I use 'this way' to turn the dog to the right and 'back' to turn left. Don't confuse the pup — teach the easier right turn first. The about turn can also be added.

All these turns are done at fast pace and are not precision turns a
taught for Obedience Showing. Just concentrate on keeping the dog'
attention and, making him turn the moment you command.

Don't try to teach the dog to
keep his head turned to watch
you as in obedience. An agility
dog needs to look where he's
going.

Later on, this heelwork can be done on the agility course, running i
and out of the obstacles.

Instant Down

A very important exercise for any dog and, one that is needed in agility
when a pause box or table is used. It can also be invaluable in preventing
a fast dog from taking the wrong course.

I like to teach the 'down' with the dog on the move, not from the sit
Have the dog on the lead walking by your side.

As you give the command
'down' run your hand down the
lead right up to the dog's neck.
Then apply gentle pressure
downwards and slightly
backwards on the lead.   At the
same time go down on one knee.
As soon as the dog is in the
'down', give lots of praise, then
have a game with him.

When you first try this, the majority of dogs will resist the pressure applied on the lead. Just keep the pressure on the lead, keeping the dog's head near the ground and, most dogs will quickly give in. Don't forget the praise.

Repeat this exercise several times at each training session and also several times when out for a walk. Always insist on instant obedience, and with a young pup especially, don't put yourself in the position of saying 'down' if you can't enforce it if necessary.

Wait on Command

In agility, with a fast dog, the handler often wants to leave him at the start and, go a couple of obstacles down the course, thus getting a head start on the dog.

Teaching this wait with a young pup, is best left until the pup can do a good sit and down stay. Don't call the pup from a stay until he is really steady at that exercise. For agility I use the command 'wait', which means 'wait until I call', rather than 'stay', which means 'stay there until I return'.

To teach the pup to stay, you need lots of patience. Start with the pup on the lead sitting beside you, and teach him to sit quietly before attempting to move away.

Once the pup is steady, give a firm 'stay' command and, take one step away to the right of the pup.

Don't step forward, as the pup is used to going forward with you doing heelwork. Don't use the pup's name with the stay command, to him the use of his name means 'come'.

Wait a few seconds then return, after standing by the pup for a few seconds, quietly praise him. Break the exercise by moving him around and having a game. If the pup moves before you return, use the lead to put him back in the sit.

Gradually increase the distance and time, always being prepared to go back to the beginning if things go wrong. Keep the training sessions short, but try to have two or three every day. Don't forget lots of praise and play. Keep it fun for the pup and, he will learn quickly.

Only when the pup is really proficient in this exercise, should you go on to teach the recall from the wait.

Recall

In agility this follows on from the wait, and later you must train the dog to do a recall over obstacles.

If you train your puppy always to come when called, this exercise should present no problems. In agility it is more a recall to heel that you need — you don't want the dog to come and sit in front of you. Rather train the dog to carry on with some fast heelwork after calling him.

Be careful of anticipation in this exercise. Sometimes return to the dog without calling him. On the agility course walk round several obstacles before going back to the dog and praising him for staying.

Send Away

It is the dog passing through the finish that stops the clock, so being able to send your dog on ahead of you is very important.

An easy way to begin training the young pup to do a send-away, is to hold the pup, put his food dish on one side of the room, then send the pup to his food from increasing distances away. Also practise send-aways to titbits and toys, having a great game afterwards.

Later, when the pup is doing a good instant down, you can sometimes
mish the send-away by downing the dog. Always remember to give lots
of praise.

On the Agility Course

As your pup gets older, if you are lucky enough to have access to an
agility course, it is very good training to practise these various control
exercises actually among the agility obstacles.

Because the pup is still working on the lead, there should be no danger
of him getting on any of the equipment.

Do fast heelwork around the obstacles, using lots of turns and altering
your speed. Put the dog down several times and make him wait.
Occasionally drop the lead and leave the pup, then call him to you. Use
lots of praise and play and keep the sessions fun.

5. READY FOR AGILITY TRAINING

Once your dog is old enough and ready for obstacle training, it is best to see if there is a club near you that holds agility classes. There are now lots of Dog Training Clubs all over the country, which teach agility. Anyone interested in beginning agility training is well advised to find a club where they can be helped to start off in the right way.

Agility is great fun if dog and handler are taught correctly. The majority of clubs do a very good job in setting handlers off on the right path.

Your local library, The Agility Club Yearbook, or **'OUR DOGS'**, will provide a list of clubs. If there isn't a club nearby, it is possible to make some equipment yourself and so still have a go.

Whether you are training at a club or by yourself, always remember the most important thing is the safety of the dog. Don't be tempted to use unsafe equipment or, attempt new things before the dog is ready. Agility is fun if taught correctly. You will never win if you overface a young dog, or get cross because your dog does something wrong. A dog that enjoys agility is a pleasure to work.

Equipment for Dog and Handler

The handler. The most important thing is good footwear, shoes that you can run in and that have a good grip, even on wet grass. Also wear clothes you can run in comfortably.

Having said 'run', don't let this word put you off having a go if you are not so agile. If you learn to control your dog at a distance, the handler will be able to take a more leisurely course.

At the moment there is a lot of interest in agility for the disabled. I think this is super and I'm sure many disabled people will be able to have a lot of fun with agility. One of the pioneers of agility for the disabled, Sheila Lane has shown that disability is no hinderance to the enjoyment of agility.

The dog. Although it is best to use some sort of training collar for heelwork practice; when you begin obstacle and jump training, use a flat leather or nylon collar, and not a check collar.

The correct collar to use for agility training.

When you are practising jumping, with the dog on the lead, an inadvertent yank with a check chain could put the dog off jumping. The check collar can be a real danger to the dog when going over obstacles, where it may get caught.

An ordinary check collar (above) or a half check collar (right), are both good for heelwork practice, but NOT for agility.

You will also require a fairly long lead made of nylon, rope or leather, not of chain, which again could get caught up.

Commands

Before beginning to train your dog, it is worth thinking about and deciding, which commands you are going to use. In agility it is best to have enough different commands to be able to tell the dog which obstacle is next. For example a dog that knows the difference between a long jump and an ordinary hurdle, or a tunnel and an 'A'-frame, is a lot less likely to get eliminated, than a dog who only knows a couple of commands.

These are the commands most commonly used.

Jumping — 'up', 'jump' and 'over'. I prefer 'up' and 'jump', to 'over' as it is easier to lift the tone of your voice with these commands.

Long jump — 'long', or 'over' (if not used for ordinary hurdles).

Tyre — 'tyre', 'hoop', 'through'.

Tunnel — 'tunnel', 'through' (if not used for the tyre). I find it is best to use a different command for the tyre and the tunnel, although the dog goes through both obstacles.

Contact obstacles — many people use the same command for all these; 'walk on', or 'plank' being the most common. You can teach your dog the difference between the see-saw and dog walk, by saying 'see-saw plank' to differentiate it from the dog walk, but it's a lot to say when out of breath. In competition it is rare to have two contact obstacles side by side, so I feel the same command is sufficient for all.

Weaving poles — 'poles', 'weave', 'in and out', 'heel and out'. I prefer the command 'weave' to the others, you are not as likely to confuse the dog (by getting the 'in' and 'out' commands in the wrong place).

Table — 'table', 'bench'.

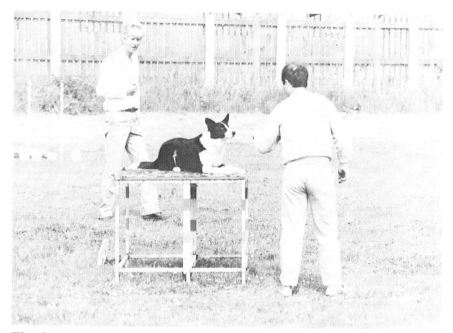

The dog has to stay down for five seconds on the table.

Directional Commands

As well as the commands for obstacles and jumping, you need directional commands to turn the dog to the right, the left, and also to send him straight ahead. I use 'this way' to turn right, 'back' to turn left and, 'go on' for straight ahead. Remember if the dog is coming towards you the commands will be reversed, e.g. 'back' will turn the dog to **your** right (the dog's left).

Commands to keep the dog on the contact points and make him wait when necessary are also important.

These are just suggestions — it doesn't really matter what you use, so long as you stick to them and don't confuse the dog. Be consistent — don't say 'up' one time and 'over' the next.

Be sure your dog understands your commands!

Praise and Play

In all the training exercises in this book the two most important words are praise and play (often referred to as p & p). I can't stress too much the importance of making sure your dog gets lots of enjoyment out of agility — so right from the start, keep it fun.

Lots of praise and
KEEP IT FUN.

6. TEACHING THE DOG TO JUMP

Equipment Needed

Three hurdles set at a height of 6" to 1' depending on the size of the dog. The hurdles should have upright stands rather than wings, which would get in the way when using the lead and, keep the handler further away from the dog. At first the jumps should be blocked in with other poles or planks, so that the dog cannot run underneath.

Stage 1.

Use one jump only and, ensure it is set up away from any other equipment, so there is nothing to distract the dog.

With the dog on the lead, run towards the centre of the jump. About 2' from the base give the command to jump, then both dog and handler jump the hurdle. Give lots of praise and play with the dog.

Repeat this several times, always jumping from the same side — never back jump at this stage.

Stage 2.

Put two jumps at least 8 paces apart, in a straight line.

Handler and dog jump number 1, praise with the voice, then carry on and both jump number 2. Praise and play.

Stage 3.

Repeat Stage 2, but after the second jump command the dog to go right, turn that way and, do a few paces of fast heelwork before praising and playing with the dog.

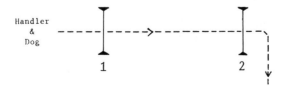

Stage 4.

Repeat Stage 2, but this time command the dog to go to the left, then turn that way and, do a few paces of fast heelwork before praise and play.

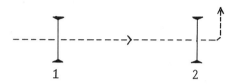

Stage 5.

Put 3 jumps in a straight line 8 paces apart. Repeat Stages 3 and 4, turning after jump 3.

Stage 6.

Handler and dog jump all three jumps, then run on a few yards and the handler puts the dog into the down position. Make it wait in the down for about 10 seconds, then praise and play.

Stage 7.

Three jumps in a straight line. Jump numbers 1 and 2, then command the dog right and, turning away from jump 3, do a few paces of fast heelwork before praise and play.

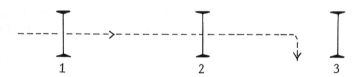

Stage 8.

Repeat Stage 7, but command the dog left and, turn left after jump 2.

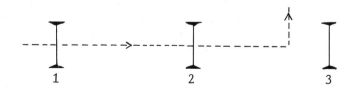

Stage 9.

Once the dog is happy and confident, work through Stages 1 to 8 again, with the handler running at the side and not jumping with the dog. Be careful the lead doesn't catch on the uprights.

Stage 10.

Three jumps in a straight line. With the dog on the lead and the handler running at the side, do all three jumps, then take the dog back to the start. Put the dog onto the handler's right and do all three jumps again, this time with the dog working on the handler's right.

I have found that the earlier you teach a dog to work on either side, the easier it is.

When the dog is happy with Stage 10, try Stages 3 to 8 with the dog working on the right.

Once the dog is happily jumping on command over blocked-in jumps, gradually remove the lower poles or planks, until the dog is jumping a single pole.

By now the dog may be ready to try off the lead. Go back to Stage 1 and, repeat all the stages off the lead. If the handler hasn't enough control and the dog runs off, put the lead back on and do more work on basic control. Never be afraid to go back to the beginning if things begin to go wrong.

As the dog becomes more confident with jumping, gradually raise the height of the jump, but try to have the dog working off the lead before attempting 2'6" high jumps. It is so easy to get the lead tangled with an upright and, give the dog an unintentional jerk. In agility training the lead should only be used if absolutely necessary.

7. TEACHING THE CONTACT OBSTACLES

These are the large pieces of equipment on an agility course, that the dog has to walk up and over. They are called contact obstacles, because the first and last 3′ of the dog-walk, see-saw and cross-over, and the first and last 3′6″ of the scale, are marked by being a different colour and are called the contact points. The dog must make contact with all of these by at least one paw, or he incurs faults. The reason for marking these contact points is that a dog jumping off these obstacles higher up, is risking injury, and is therefore not doing the obstacle correctly.

Scale or 'A' Frame

This is the first contact obstacle that I teach. I find it is usually the easiest for the beginner dog, although many handlers won't believe this. I'm sure it is the width of the plank that you are asking them to walk up that bothers a dog, not the height, and a 3′ wide scale is a lot less formidable looking to a dog than a 9″ dog walk plank.

If you are lucky enough to have access to a lower training scale, this is a great help. My scale can be lowered so the apex is about 4′ high.

This enables the beginner dog to be held by the collar and, helped over the top of the obstacle. Holding the collar gives the handler a lot more control and problems rarely occur.

An assistant on the opposite side, ensures the dog stays in the centre of the scale.

If introducing a dog to this obstacle using a full height scale (apex 6′3″), I have found the following method best. With a flat leather or nylon collar fastened fairly tightly, so it won't slip over the dog's head, attach two leads to the dog. The handler holds one and the trainer or assistant holds the other. It is best if the handler works on the side he is most used to and the assistant on the other.

Start about 2 yards away from the base of the scale — the dog doesn't need a very long run, and walk smartly forward giving the command decided upon.

Keep both leads taut and assist the dog up, over and down. By keeping the leads taut you prevent the dog jumping off at the side. On the first attempt resistance may be met, usually just before the top. If at all possible, insist that the dog continues by using a third person standing behind, to give a gentle push to the dog if necessary.

Don't let the dog turn round and go back down. Repeat this procedure from the same side two or three times.

If the handler is very tall, holding the dog by the collar gives more control.

With the occasional dog who seems very nervous of the scale, it may help to place a table at the side for the handler to stand on, so that he is closer to the dog when he is at the top. As a last resort, the handler (if agile enough), can sit on top of the scale and call the dog up. Be careful to leave enough room at the side of the handler, for the dog to get over.

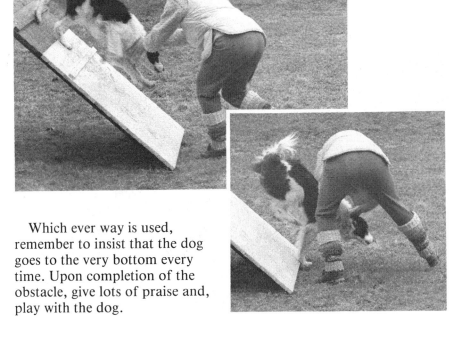

Which ever way is used, remember to insist that the dog goes to the very bottom every time. Upon completion of the obstacle, give lots of praise and, play with the dog.

The first time a dog is introduced to this obstacle, 3 or 4 successful attempts are sufficient — don't go on and on, getting the dog tired and fed up.

As soon as you are confident that the dog will go straight over and not turn round or jump off at the side, do this obstacle off the lead. To begin with you may need to catch hold of the dog's collar and, guide him onto the obstacle. The sooner you can leave the lead off the better. Using the lead, (especially only one lead), there is always the risk of it getting caught over the top and, unintentionally jerking the dog.

At this stage of training, never let the dog turn round after the scale and go back over. Always go round and do the same side again or, do another obstacle before going back over the scale. In competition it only needs one paw to be put back on the scale, and you may be eliminated for taking the wrong course.

Dog Walk

A dog walk with a height of about 2′ is excellent for training the beginner dog. Many clubs convert old, full sized dog walks to training height when they get a new one. The dog walk I have, is designed to adjust to any height between 2′ and 4′6″ and this is very useful.

With a dog that seems very nervous of this obstacle, I have on occasion, removed one plank and placed it on bricks about 6″ high. This gets the dog used to walking on the plank first. This can help, but it is difficult to prevent the dog stepping off, when the plank is so near to the ground.

The training method is the same whatever the height of the dog walk, but obviously it is easier when lower, particularly with a heavy dog.

When introducing this obstacle have an assistant on the opposite side to the handler.

Stage 1 — pick up the dog (if possible) and place him halfway down the down plank of the dog walk, facing downwards. Let the dog stand still for a few seconds, praising all the time. Then, holding the dog by the collar and with the assistant walking at the other side, encourage the dog to walk quietly down and off, (to the very bottom of course). Give lots of praise and repeat this stage two or three times or, until the dog is quite happy.

Stage 2 — place the dog at the top of the down plank and repeat Stage 1. Do this several times, again giving lots of praise.

Stage 1

Stage 2

Stage 3 — place the dog in the centre of the top plank, still facing the same way. Some dogs sit — this doesn't matter. Let him sit for a few seconds, then using the collar again, encourage him to walk down. The assistant may need to hold the dog on the other side. New handlers must be watched to make sure they don't accidentally pull the dog off.

Stage 4 — when the dog is quite happy going down and off, take him round and do the complete obstacle. Still face the same direction, so that the dog is taking the down plank he is used to.

Once the dog seems happy and secure, hold the collar to start him up the plank. Release the collar until the dog reaches the end of the down

plank, when you may need to hold him onto the contact.

I am not happy when handlers, particularly beginner handlers, allow the dog to attempt the dog walk on the lead. It is so easy to pull a dog off balance, and a fall at this stage can really set a dog back. An experienced handler should always be present to help during early training.

The Cross-Over or Dog Cross

To a dog proficient on the dog walk, this obstacle should present no real problems.

The handler must learn to control the direction of the dog on the top, and may need to make him wait, or even lie down, on the centre.

The See-Saw

Preliminary training. Under very careful supervision, I have found it a big help to rock a young puppy on the see-saw. This is **not** letting him do the obstacle. The pup is placed in the centre and held there, while an

assistant very gently moves the plank up and down, then the pup is lifted off. While holding the pup, the handler praises him, and after lifting him down plays with him. Pups I have done this with seem to have no trouble with the see-saw later, but it must be carefully supervised so that there is no risk to the pup.

I never introduce an older dog to the see-saw until he is quite happy on the dog walk. To a dog, a see-saw is a small dog walk that suddenly moves.

To introduce a dog to the see-saw, you need an assistant holding the plank so that it can't bang down even if the handler lets the dog go too far or too fast.

The handler, holding the dog's collar, walks him quietly up to the centre of the plank. This should present no difficulty if the dog is happy

doing the dog walk. Once at the centre, stop the dog and make him wait, don't worry if he sits. After a few seconds, having praised him for waiting, encourage the dog to step forward. His weight should by now be starting to tip the plank. The assistant lets the plank go slowly down to the ground, while the handler, still holding the dog, praises and encourages.

Only when the plank is actually on the ground, does the handler walk the dog down and off. This needs to be repeated several times with lots of praise afterwards.

As the dog gets more proficient and learns to wait in the centre, the handler can loose the dog. He should still catch hold of the plank and help it down, until the dog has learnt to control the tip for himself.

In competition a dog may be given 5 faults if the see-saw does not touch the ground before he gets off, even if he touched the contact point. A dog that 'flies' off the see-saw is not doing the obstacle correctly and, is in danger of serious injury. It is well worth teaching your dog to wait on the see-saw.

The actual spot where you want to make the dog wait, differs with the size and conformation of the dog. You need to work out just where to stop your dog, so that he can control the tip.

The lighter the dog, the further he will need to go.

With all the contact obstacles take it steady and, teach the dog to do the obstacles correctly and safely. Speed will follow later. In training always make a dog go as far down the contact as possible — in the excitement of competition you will rarely get so far down.

8. WEAVING POLES

This is one of the hardest obstacles in agility. A dog who is accurate and fast at weaving has a real advantage. Many a class has been won by skill in weaving, so it is well worth teaching this carefully. A row of poles (between 5 to 12) of a minimum height 2'6", are fixed in (or on) the ground 18" — 24" apart. The dog has to enter with the first pole on his left and, must weave in and out along the line without missing any poles. Any mistakes in the poles must be corrected before going on to the next obstacle.

There are several ways of teaching the poles, what works with one dog may not work with another. I have taught a number of different dogs to weave and, I've learnt something new with each one.

I don't believe you should bend the dog until he is at least 11 months old, but you can teach the speed well before that.

Both the following methods of teaching the poles teach the speed first. You can start training when the pup is about 6 months old.

Method One

This method was taught to me by Peter Lewis.
Equipment needed — 12 poles and 10 wires 4' long. The poles are arranged like this.

Each wire joins two poles spaced 4' apart. The wires are straight and set at a height of about 2" below the dog's shoulder. The distance apart of each pole is twice the normal, you start with the two lines about 18" apart. As training progresses move the poles together very gradually, until they are just a dog's width apart. They stay at this width until the dog is old enough to bend.

It is important to use an equal number of poles on each line, so that the dog can go from either end. It is also vital to have the first pole on the left line, so that the dog learns to enter correctly. In agility the dog must enter the poles with the first one on his left.

With the poles set out like this, work through the following exercises.
1. With the dog on the lead, run him through the poles using the command decided upon right from the start. Give lots of praise and play (p.&p).
2. Leave the dog right in the entrance to the poles, held if necessary by an assistant. Walk through the poles to the end, turn and call the dog to you, still using the weave command as well as 'come', p&p.

NB. For clarity in the following photographs string was used instead of wire.

3. With the dog waiting at the start, go and put a toy or titbit at the end of the poles. Return to the dog and send him through the poles to the toy or titbit, p.&p.

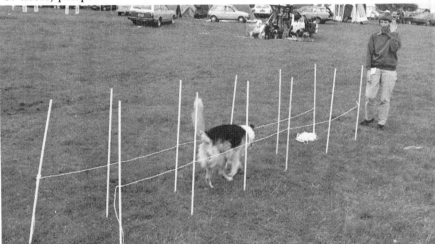

4. If your aim is good enough, throw the toy, making sure it lands in line with the poles. Send the dog to fetch the toy, then call the dog back through the poles, p.&p.

5.　If training an older dog with this method, put a small jump a few yards from the end of the poles and, put the toy after the jump. Send the dog through the poles and over the jump to collect the toy, he then returns over the jump and through the poles, p.&p.

6.　As the dog's training progresses and he can do a steady wait, leave the dog at the start. Go and place the toy, return to the dog and let him go to fetch it. This wait will make the dog more eager to go.

With all these exercises, make a big thing of the poles and get the dog really keen. Give lots of praise and play afterwards. Doing this two or three times a day for just a few minutes each time, will soon make a pup love the poles. Don't forget to use the weave command each time.

Because string was used instead of wire, extra (dark) poles were added to illustrate the bend.

When the dog is old enough to bend and, has had lots of this preliminary training, very slowly bend the wires and move the poles in closer together. This process should not be rushed, only move the poles 1/2" at a time.

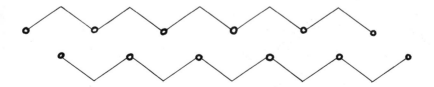

As the poles move slowly in, the dog has to begin to bend to get through them. Work through exercises 2 — 6 several times, each time you move the poles. Don't rush this stage or the dog will jump out over the wires. N.B. The dark poles would be absent when wire is used.

At last the poles will be in a straight line, still with the wires attached. You may need to increase the length of the wires to get maximum bend yet keep the distance between poles at 18″.

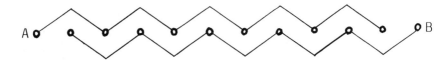

Continue training with these for quite a time until the dog is really proficient. Then gradually remove the wires, beginning with the centre ones and leaving wires A and B until last.

Don't be in a hurry to remove wires A and B, these ensure correct entry into the poles.

Method Two

I was taught this method by Malcolm Bassett.
Equipment needed — 12 poles.
 With this method the bases of the poles are in a straight line, but the poles are angled out at either side.

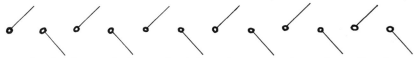

 Again the first pole is on the left and, an equal number of poles are used.

 At first the poles are placed only about 9″ above horizontal and, as in method one, the dog can run straight through. With the poles set like this, all the exercises from Method One can be worked through.

 When the dog is old enough to bend, the poles are very slowly moved upright and, the dog begins to bend without really noticing.

Both these methods teach the speed first. Other methods can also be successful. Bending the dog round normally spaced poles on the lead, or using a toy or titbit to make him go in and out can work, but then the speed has to be built up later. Sometimes a combination of methods is necessary.

I began to train Heidi, my Border Collie, using Method One when she was 6 months. It was very successful until I began to bend the wires. No matter how slight the bend was, as soon as she felt any resistance from the wire, instead of bending, she jumped out. I changed to Method Two. Again, while she could run straight through them it was fine, and Heidi was soon tearing through these poles. As soon as they were more upright and she had to push against them however, she just ran out.

Finally, I went back to the way I originally taught Riki, my Sheltie — having the poles as in competition and using a toy or titbit to guide the dog through. After only a few days of this the penny dropped and Heidi was away. She had realised what I wanted and now all that earlier speed training paid off. Very soon she could weave at speed through normally spaced poles.

It was a combination of methods that worked with Heidi, but I'm sure it was that early speed training which has made her so keen to get through the poles and, has made her love weaving so much.

Once your dog is weaving well, you want to get him used to entering correctly from every different angle and, entering by himself if possible.

It takes time to teach the poles, even after the dog has learnt, lots of practise is necessary before the dog will be really proficient.

Heidi weaves really well now, but it was 12 months after she had begun competing before I could trust her to enter the poles correctly by herself. Before then I had to make her wait for me to catch up and, show her which poles to go in. After a further 6 months' practice, she would do the poles with me on the opposite side if necessary.

The dog enters and completes the poles correctly, even with it's handler standing on the opposite side.

Don't give up at the first problem. You will get there in the end, and a dog that weaves well is super to watch. Remember that the most important thing is to keep weaving fun for the dog.

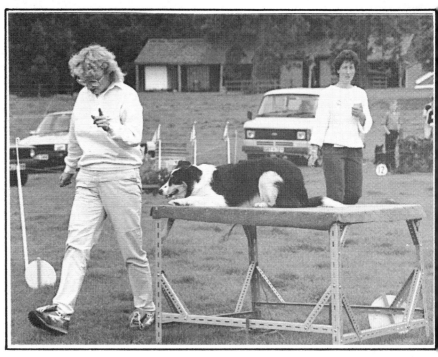

9. OTHER OBSTACLES

Pause Box

Rarely used in competition these days, but a very useful exercise to teach the dog anyway.

A pause box is usually 4′ square and, if you haven't a wooden one, simply fix four pieces of tape to the ground. Keep the box in the same place for each training session.

Decide which command you are going to use — I like the command 'box', followed by 'down' when the dog is in the box. When he knows the 'box' command a dog will look for the box, a help when ahead of the handler.

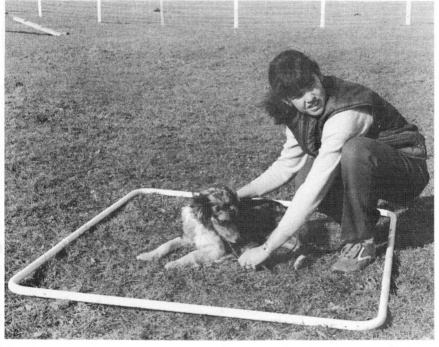

1. Run up with the dog on the lead, giving the box command and pointing it out to the dog. Once there, put the dog down in the box and, give plenty of p.&p.

Repeat this several times.

2.   Making the dog wait a few yards away from the box, go and crouch down just behind or in the box. Call the dog, then give the 'box' command, followed by 'down' when the dog gets to the box, p.&p.

The handler calls the dog to the box, using a toy to encourage it.

3.   Let the dog see you put a toy or titbit into the box.

Send the dog to it from a few yards away. The handler runs up behind, downs the dog and, gives lots of p.&p. The dog will probably eat the titbit (if used), before going down.

4. Pretend to put a titbit or toy in the box. Send the dog. The handler follows closely behind to give the titbit or toy as soon as the dog is down in the box, p.&p.

5. When the dog is going happily to the box, send him without putting or pretending to put a titbit or toy there. Be sure to give lots of praise when the dog is down in the box.

6. With a dog old enough to jump, place a hurdle in line with the box and, repeat these various stages with the dog doing the jump first.

Table

Unless using a low training table, I like a dog to be happy jumping 2'6" before introducing it to this obstacle.

There are two training aids useful when teaching a dog to jump onto the table.

The first is to put a smaller table or firmly fixed board beside the table, approximately half the height. The dog then uses this as a stepping stone. The second, which can be used in conjunction with the first, is to place a piece of carpet over the table, so that it hangs down one side to cover the gap. This gap, if uncovered, seems to put a number of dogs off when they first attempt the table.

Approach the table with the dog on the lead, give the chosen command and using the lead, assist the dog to jump up onto the table. At first it may help to use the 'jump' command as well, but drop this as soon as possible.

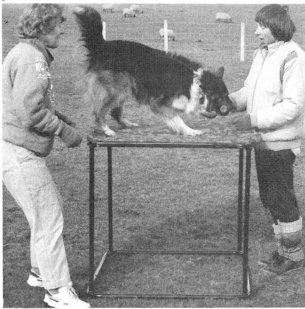

Once the dog is on the table, give lots of p.&p. Don't insist on downing the dog at this stage, get it happy with jumping onto the table. Once the dog is happy doing this on the lead, try it off, but still run up with the dog. Later put a titbit or toy on the table and, send the dog from a few yards away.

A really nervous dog, (nervous of the table that is), may be helped by the handler kneeling on the table and calling him, while an assistant handles the dog.

I find getting the dog onto the table is rarely a problem. The bigger problem can be making the dog lie down on it. I like a beginner handler to be able to make their dog go down on command on the ground, before trying this on the table.

One point to watch out for: the handler says 'down', and then finds their dog jumps back off the table. Often they are using this command to get their dog off the furniture at home — in this case use a different command such as 'flat'.

Another problem: the dog that rushes the table and slides straight off. In this case teach the dog to wait before jumping onto the table. It sometimes helps to say 'wait' or 'stay' as the dog lands, before giving the 'down' command.

Once the dog is happy lying down on the table, the handler should walk right round the table or, over to an obstacle and back, to make sure the dog remains quite steady.

In training, when doing a 5 second count, never let your dog go, on the command 'go'. Make it wait a few more seconds or, you will soon have a dog that anticipates the count in competition.

Tunnels

These rarely give much trouble unless very wet. Once used to tunnels many dogs love them so much, that the problem can be keeping them out of the tunnel when they should be doing another obstacle.

The tunnel is the one obstacle I allow a young pup to do. Most of my dogs have learnt by following an older dog through. Young pups don't seem to have the fear of dark places that some older dogs possess and, they love this training.

The young puppy follows an older dog through the tunnel, first the collapsible, then the pipe.

64

When introducing tunnels to an older dog, I have found it usually best to use the collapsible tunnel first. This is for two reasons — many dogs dislike the sound and feel of their claws on the pipe tunnel at first and also, the collapsible tunnel can be rolled up, so that the dog only has a short distance to go through. All right, you can push the pipe tunnel together, but I still find most dogs prefer the collapsible one.

An assistant holds the dog at the entrance while the handler goes to the end of the tunnel, rolls it back and, holds it up, whilst looking through the tunnel to see the dog, before calling him. The lead can be passed through the tunnel to the handler.

Try to be sure the dog is looking at the handler before he is called, or he may try to run round the side.

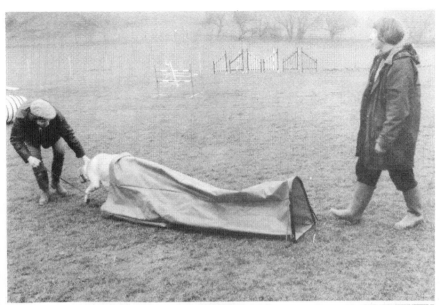

Give lots of praise as soon as the dog reaches the handler and repeat several times, extending the length of the tunnel as the dog gets used to it.

I have found that most dogs are quite happy after a session of this and then, usually go through the pipe tunnel with no trouble.

If there is a problem with a very nervous dog, it is quite possible and amusing, for the handler to go through the pipe tunnel with the dog.

The length of the tunnel is extended as the dog gets used to it. A second helper raises the top of the tunnel during the early stages.

Once the dog is going through the tunnel happily, the handler should try to send him through without the help of an assistant. When doing this, be sure the dog is well into the tunnel before running on and calling him or, the dog may turn round and come back out.

Whenever using the collapsible tunnel be sure it is straight before sending the dog through. A dog that gets tangled up in the tunnel may panic and, be put off tunnels for a time.

Tyre

Introduce the beginner dog to this obstacle with the tyre fixed, or held as near to the ground as possible, so that the dog is not given the chance to go underneath.

Decide which command you are going to use; I don't like using the 'jump' command as the dog may well try to jump the whole obstacle. The usual commands are 'hoop', 'tyre' or 'through'.

The lead is passed through the tyre and, the handler calls the dog through.

With an assistant holding the dog right up close to the tyre, the handler goes to stand on the other side. Using his hands to show the dog where to jump through, he calls the dog, giving the tyre command as well as 'come'.

A titbit can be shown to the dog through the hole, the hand and titbit moving back as the dog begins to jump. Once through, lots of p.&p. and, the titbit if used. This should be repeated until the dog is quite happy doing it. The handler can then send the dog through without assistance. At this stage never let the dog jump back through the tyre, rather take him round and do it from the same side or, do another obstacle in between.

Once the dog is going through a low tyre happily, the tyre should be raised gradually. Often this is not possible, and the dog has to go from a very low tyre to the normal height. In this case, it helps to block the gap under the tyre to begin with. Go back to having an assistant holding the dog, with the handler calling him through, until the dog is quite confident at full height.

The gap under the full height tyre is blocked off at first.

Once the dog is jumping through the tyre at full height, never lower or raise it. The dog gets used to this height and can misjudge, with the risk of injury, if the height is altered.

With a beginner dog and even an advanced dog, be sure to line the dog up straight before sending him through the tyre. Hopefully this will prevent the dog jumping through the side and, ensure safe passage through the tyre.

Long Jump

When first introducing the long jump I put the boards on their edges to a length of about 3'. By doing this the dog is discouraged from walking on the boards.

What NOT to teach the dog. This Jack Russell sees the long jump as a line of stepping stones!

I also put a low hurdle (15″ high) in the middle of the boards. With this hurdle in, there is no need to put corner poles, which will get in the handler's way if using the lead. By using a hurdle in the middle, the dog is jumping something he is used to and also, you are training for height over the long jump. A dog who only skims the long jump is always liable to knock the last board over.

With the boards on their sides and, a hurdle in the centre, he jumps well.

First run up with the dog on the lead. Give the usual 'jump' command and using the lead, lift the dog slightly over the jump, p.&p. Now the dog knows he's got to jump. Repeat this, but begin using the command for the long jump. I like a different command, usually 'long'. At first it may be necessary to use both commands, but drop the 'jump' one as soon as possible.

When the dog is happy at this length, gradually increase the length up to 5′ (3′ for mini's), still with the boards on their edges and, with a hurdle in the centre.

Finally stand the boards up, the middle one first, gradually righting the others, so that the dog is not suddenly presented with five stepping stones.

Once doing the long jump off the lead and without the hurdle, put in four corner posts to prevent cross jumping.

The boards are righted gradually, centre one first.

Here three boards are standing up. Note the good height the dog is getting over the hurdle.

All the boards are upright now, but the dog still has the hurdle, to encourage height.

When the hurdle is finally removed, corner poles are added to prevent cross jumping.

10. DIFFERENT TYPES OF HURDLES

Once jumping happily, the dog should have as much experience of different types of hurdles as possible. When he then meets a strange looking jump in a competition, he will be quite happy to have a go. Try to get experience of jumping all the following.

Parallel Planks

Not usually a problem, unless too sturdy looking and the dog banks them (i.e. stands on top).

Gate

This usually has a top pole and should be quite simple for the dog.

Brush

Should have an easily displaceable top unit — generally a pole. A brush fence rarely has wings so watch that the dog doesn't run out.

Wall

Should have displaceable bricks on the top. As this obstacle is quite inviting for a dog to bank, I like a dog to be really confident at jumping 2'6" before tackling a wall.

In training insist that the dog jumps clear, don't accept a foot on the top, even if the brick stays there — do the obstacle again correctly.

Single Pole

Always train a dog to jump a single pole, then you know he is really jumping on command, and not just because there is an obstacle in the way. I do most of my training with single pole jumps. Should the dog run underneath, lowering the jump and then making him do it a few times on the lead, usually cures it. Also putting a pole on the ground beneath the jump helps, because it gives the dog a ground line.

Spread

Two single hurdles are placed together to form a spread. When both hurdles are set at the same height, the spread must not exceed 2'. If the top pole on the first hurdle is at least 6" lower than the second, the maximum spread may be 2'6".

When training, always have a second low pole on the first hurdle to give the dog a ground line. Introduce the spread at a height of no more than 2', with a 6" lower front pole, before trying a parallel spread.

I find the easiest way to introduce a spread is to use a short long jump (about 3') and, put the spread over it. The dog has a good ground line with the front board of the long jump and, is used to jumping the length.

Starting at about 18" high and 1' apart, gradually increase the height of the spread, always raising the back pole first. Also slowly increase the width between the two hurdles, until the dog is jumping a 2' spread.

Finally remove the long jump, replacing it with a low pole to give a
ground line. I find that spreads taught this way are rarely a problem.
Some people find it helps their dog to use a slightly different command to
tell him that it is a spread.

Water Jump

This is just a different looking long jump, and should be treated as
such.

Wishing Well

This has a displaceable top bar. There can be two problems with the well. Firstly the dog may dislike jumping under a roof — in this case it may help to use the command for 'through' rather than 'jump'. Secondly, it is very easy for the dog to stand on the well and earn 5 faults, even if he doesn't knock the pole down.

Make sure your dog is quite happy at jumping 2′6″ and can do spreads, before attempting the well. Give the dog enough run, don't let him try to jump it from a standstill, as that is asking for the dog to stand on it.

The dog will earn 5 faults if he stands on the well, even if he doesn't knock the pole down.

When first teaching this obstacle, I put a hurdle against the front, with a pole at the height of the top of the well base, and another at the bottom to give a ground line. This makes the well resemble the spreads the dog is used to jumping, thus discouraging him from standing on the well.

11. JUMPING EXERCISES AND CONTROL TRAINING

The following set of exercises can be used for the beginner dog, with the jumps set as low as 6″. Big dogs will probably need them at 1′ to prevent them just stepping over.

These exercises done at full height with a more advanced dog, are excellent control training. They will help to make the dog handy over jumps and, pay attention to the handler.

With the beginner dog, several poles can be used on the jumps to prevent the dog going underneath. With the more experienced dog it is best to work towards using single poles.

All the exercises can be done with the dog on the left or right of the handler, but some flow much better with the dog on one specific side. When applicable, I indicate the handling position I consider the most appropriate, but you should experiment and use that most suited to your dog.

As with all agility training, be conscious of safety. Move all other obstacles far enough away, so that there is no danger to the dog of collision, or distraction from the exercise being taught. Jumps used, must be jumped from both sides, so make sure that the poles can be knocked off from either side.

It is not necessarily intended for all the stages of one exercise to be done at the same training session. But it is easier to explain all the variations at the same time. How much you cover each session depends on your dog. Some dogs can take a lot of training happily, while others get bored. Never try to do too much and, keep it fun. Always end with something the dog can do and enjoys, and remember, lots of praise and play, (p.&p.).

Exercise 1

Aim of exercise — to teach the dog to jump at the handler's command, not just because there is an obstacle in front of him. Also training the dog to work either side of the handler.

Equipment — circle of 4 jumps set at 3 o'clock, 6, 9 and 12 o'clock, with at least 8 paces between.

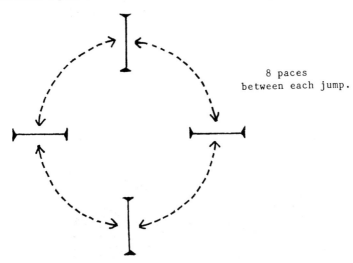

```
8 paces
between each jump.
```

1.   Run clockwise round the circle, the dog jumps each hurdle in turn, working on the handler's left, p.&p.
2.   Run anti-clockwise, the dog jumps each hurdle, working on the handler's right, p.&p.
   If the dog is very unsure working on the right, run this a few times first, with the dog on the left — the handler has much further to run this way.
3.   Run clockwise with the dog on the handler's left. Run up to each jump, command the dog to 'wait', checking if necessary. Wait a few seconds, then command him to 'jump', and do the hurdle, p.&p.
4.   Repeat 3, running anti-clockwise, with the dog on the handler's right.
5.   Running clockwise with the dog on the left, jump 1, make the dog wait for a few seconds in front of jump 2, then jump 2 & 3, make the dog wait before jumping 4, p.&p.
6.   Running clockwise with the dog on the left, jump 1, call the dog to heel and miss out jump 2, running past quite close to the jump, jump 3, miss out jump 4, p.&p.
7.   Repeat 5 and 6, running anti-clockwise with the dog on the handler's right. Jumps will be done in reverse order, p.&p.

8. Running clockwise, run round 1, jump 2 & 3, run round 4, p.&p.
9. Running clockwise, jump 1 & 2, miss out 3, jump 4, p.&p.
10. Running clockwise, jump 1, miss out 2 & 3, jump 4, p.&p.
11. Repeat 8-10, running anti-clockwise, with the dog on the handler's right, p.&p.

When missing out a jump, run towards it and, when about a yard away, just before the point where the dog would take off, command the dog sharply to heel and run round the jump. If the dog still jumps, don't tell him off, simply repeat but give the heel command earlier.

Exercise 2
KEY TO FIGURES

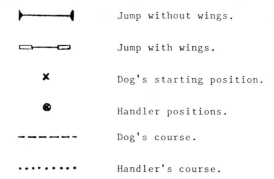

├──────┤   Jump without wings.

▭──────▭   Jump with wings.

✗   Dog's starting position.

❽   Handler positions.

–– –– –––   Dog's course.

••••••••   Handler's course.

Aim of exercise — to teach directional control and, back jumping on command only.

Equipment — one hurdle. Practise on a hurdle with wings and also one without.

1.   Send the dog over the jump. As he jumps, command him to turn right, and moving over to the right of the jump, call the dog to you, past, not over the jump, p.&p. Repeat several times.

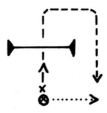

2.   Send the dog over the jump. As he jumps, command him to turn left, and moving over to the left, call the dog to you, past, not over the jump, p.&p. Repeat several times.

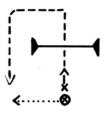

3.   Send the dog over the jump. Move up close to the jump and call the dog back over the jump, p.&p. Decide which command to use for back jumping. If you use 'back' to turn the dog left, don't use it for back jumping. I use the command '& again'.

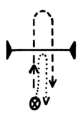

Once the dog really understands the directional commands, use stages 1, 2 & 3 in various combinations. Also work towards being able to call the dog back to you past the jump, but without having to move far to the side. Work out just where to give the command to turn. Some dogs can turn in the air, while others will land first. If you give the command too early, you may turn the dog before the jump or, make it mistime its take off, and land on the jump.

Once the dog is proficient at this exercise, repeat it using the tyre. Numbers 1 and 2 can also be done with the long jump, but obviously not stage 3.

Exercise 3

Aim of exercise — to teach the dog to wait, then return to the handler over the jumps. Also more directional control.

Equipment — row of 3 winged jumps. With a beginner dog, have the jumps about 8 paces apart and at half height. As training progresses, raise the jumps and move them closer until they are 5 paces apart (never less).

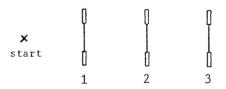

1. Run, with the dog jumping all 3, p.&p.
2. Leave the dog at the start (held if necessary). The handler steps over jump 1, (not round as the dog may follow the handler's scent), and turns to face the dog. Standing close to the jump, the handler shows the dog where to jump, and calls him over, p.&p.
3. Repeat stage 2, but with the handler stepping over, and calling the dog over two jumps, p.&p. With more advanced dogs, stages 2 & 3 can be left out.
4. Repeat stage 2, but the handler now walks round the jump not over it. Still stand close to the jump to call the dog, but move back as the dog jumps.
5. Repeat 4 over two jumps.
    When the dog is happy and confident with these stages, try the following.
6. Leave the dog, stand between jumps 1 & 2 on the right. Call the dog over jump 1, as he lands command him to turn right, then do a few paces of heelwork, going away to the right, p.&p.

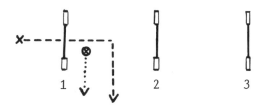

7.   Leave the dog, stand between jumps 2 & 3 on the right. Call the dog over 1 & 2, command him to turn right, do heelwork as in 6, p.&p.

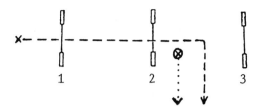

8.   Leave the dog, stand between jumps 1 & 2 on the left. Call the dog over jump 1, give the command to turn left and heelwork as before, p.&p. This is best done with the dog on the handler's right.

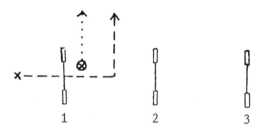

9.   Leave the dog, stand between jumps 2 & 3 on the left. Call the dog over 1 & 2, command him to turn left and heelwork as before, p.&p.

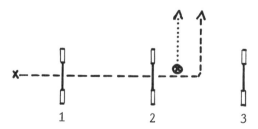

10. More advanced dogs can practise being called over three jumps. When turning them right or left, it would be a good idea to add a fourth jump to the line, so that the dog can be turned away from it.

With this exercise, and any others where you leave your dog at the start, be careful to line him up with the jump and, leave him far enough back. Many dogs knock the first fence down in competition, because their handlers leave them too close.

If you are working the dog on the right, as in stages 8 & 9, put him on the right before leaving him. Don't walk across in front, which can be confusing to a beginner dog. By leaving him on the right, you are warning the dog of your intention. At first you could even face the dog slightly to the way you want him to turn, — only slightly, or you risk him wing jumping or running round the jump.

When making the dog wait, occasionally return and praise the dog without calling him, so preventing anticipation.

Notes

Exercise 4

Aim of exercise — teaching the dog the send away over jumps, to a table or pause box. This also teaches the dog to go through finish posts.

Equipment — row of 3 winged jumps, pause box or table, 2 finish poles. Set the jumps 8 paces apart at first, move them closer as the dog progresses, but no closer than 5 paces. The table or pause box should be a similar distance from the last jump. The finish poles are placed as shown.

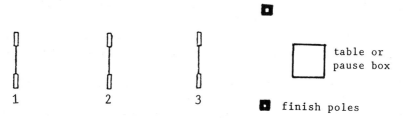

table or pause box

finish poles

1. Run, with the dog jumping all three jumps and, give the table command. Put the dog down on the table, wait a few seconds, then praise and play with the dog while he is still on the table. Repeat this several times.

2. Leave the dog in front of jump 3, go and stand by the table. Call the dog over the jump and onto the table, p.&p.

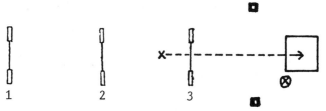

3. Let the dog watch you put a toy or titbit onto the table. Repeat stage 2. Let the dog eat the titbit or, have a game with the toy.

4. Making sure the dog sees, leave a toy or titbit on the table. Stand with the dog in front of jump 3. Send the dog over the jump and onto the table. Follow the dog to the table but hang back a little, so that the dog is going ahead, p.&p.

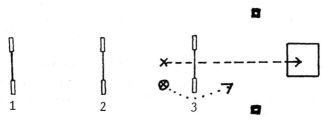

5. Repeat 4, with the handler staying in front of jump 3 until the dog is on the table. Command him to go down, then go to the table p.&p.
6. Repeat 5 but without putting the toy or titbit on the table. Run up after the dog is down, and give a titbit or have a game with the toy.
7. Repeat stages 4, 5 & 6 starting in front of jump 2.
8. If the dog is confident enough, repeat stages 4, 5 & 6, starting in front of jump 1.

It may take several weeks to get the dog going over a number of jumps. Make haste slowly is the best advice. Never be afraid to go back a few stages if the dog lacks confidence.

Use jumps with wings at first, so that the dog is less likely to run out at the side. When the dog is really confident, try him on jumps without wings.

When the dog is happy being sent on, and is doing a good reliable 'down' on the table, try the following.
9. Start in front of jump 1. Send the dog over all three jumps and, 'down' him on the table for at least 10 seconds. While the dog is down, the handler moves to stand in front of jump 3. Call the dog off the table and over 3, p.&p.

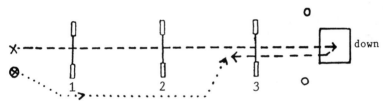

10. Repeat 9, but after the dog has jumped 3, run the dog back to the start, with him jumping back over 2 & 1 in turn, p.&p.

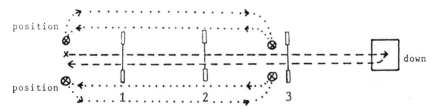

With the handler starting in position 1, as shown in the diagram, the dog would be working on the right when running back to the start. Starting in position 2, the dog would be working on the handler's left coming back. Practise both ways.
11. Start in front of jump 1. Send the dog over the three jumps to the table, 'down' him for 10 seconds. The handler moves to stand in front of jump 2. Recall the dog over 3 and 2, and run with him as he jumps 1 and goes back to the start, p.&p.

12. Start in front of jump 1. Send the dog over all three jumps to the table, 'down' him for 10 seconds. The handler remains at the start and recalls the dog over all three jumps, p.&p.

The pause box can be used instead of the table in this exercise. I find it is easier using the table, because it is a more definite obstacle for the dog to aim at. Probably it is best to use the table at first and later, when the dog is used to going away, try the exercise with a pause box.

If you have included finish poles in this exercise, the dog will have got used to going through them. Now remove the table or pause box and, using a toy or titbit placed on the ground beyond the poles, train the dog to go on through the poles alone.

Exercise 5

Aim of exercise — directional control and paying attention to the handler.

Equipment — square of jumps 8 paces apart.

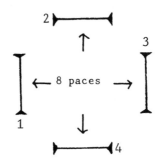

1. Jump 1 then 3, p.&p.

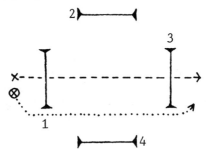

2. With the dog on the handler's left, jump 1. Command the dog to turn right, jump 4, p.&p.

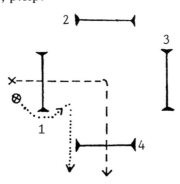

3. With the dog on the handler's right, jump 1. Command the dog to turn left, jump 2, p.&p.

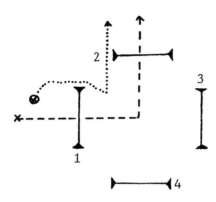

4. With the dog on the handler's left, leave him at the start. The handler stands between 1 & 3, calls the dog over 1, sends him on over 3, and commands the dog to turn right. The handler runs to stand between jumps 3 & 4 and makes the dog jump 4 from the back, p.&p. Make sure that the dog goes far enough out to have room to jump 4 safely.

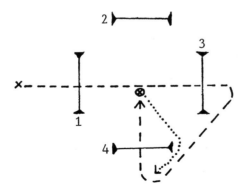

5. With the dog on the handler's right, leave him at the start. The handler stands between 1 & 3, calls the dog over 1, sends him on over 3, and commands the dog to turn left. The handler stands between 2 & 3 and makes the dog jump 2 from the back, p.&p.

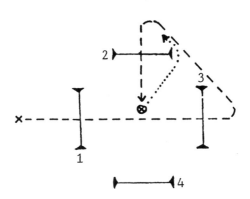

6. With the dog on the handler's left, leave him at the start. The handler stands in the centre of the jumps, calls the dog over 1, sends him on over 3, and commands the dog right. Call him in between jumps 3 & 4, command him to go left and jump 4 from the front, p.&p.

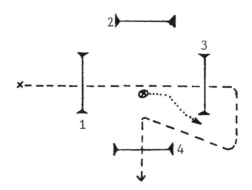

7.   With the dog on the handler's right, leave him at the start. The handler stands in the centre of the jumps, calls the dog over 1, sends him on over 3, and commands the dog left. Call him in between jumps 3 & 2, command him to go right and jump 2 from the front, p.&p.

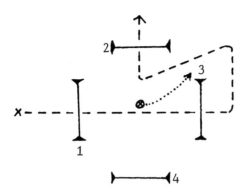

8.   Leave the dog at the start. The handler stands behind 3, and calls the dog over 1 & 3, p.&p.

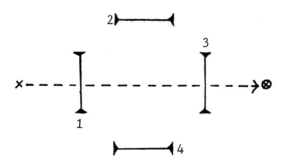

9. Leave the dog in front of 2. The handler stands behind 4 and, calls the dog over 2 & 4, p.&p.

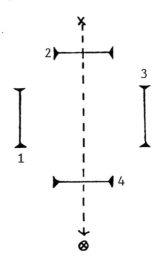

These last two simple stages could be done at anytime during this exercise, so that the dog does not think he's always going to turn.

Exercise 6

Aim of exercise — to teach directional control and, returning to the handler past the jumps, not always over them.

Equipment — 3 hurdles in a line, with 1 yard between each. Use jumps without wings initially, but as the dog progresses try the same exercise with winged jumps.

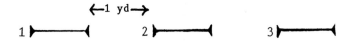

1.   Send the dog over jump 2, turn to the right and call him back over jump 3, p.&p. Repeat several times.

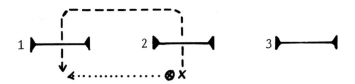

2.   Send the dog over jump 2, turn to the left and call him back over jump 1, p.&p. Repeat several times.

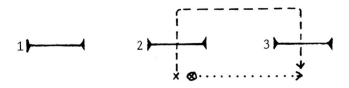

3.   Send the dog over jump 1, command him to turn right, call him back over jump 2, command him to turn left and send him over jump 3, p.&p.

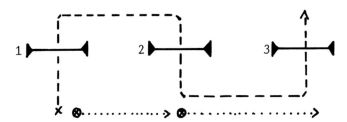

4.   Send the dog over jump 3, command him to turn left, call him back over jump 2, command him to turn right and send him over jump 1, p.&p.

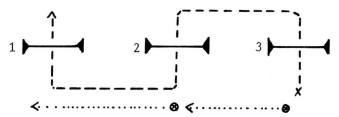

5.   Send the dog over jump 1, command him to turn right. The handler moves to stand between jumps 1 & 2 and calls the dog back between the jumps, p.&p.

6.   Send the dog over jump 2, command him to turn left. The handler moves to stand between jumps 2 & 1 and calls the dog back between the jumps, p.&p.

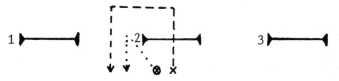

As the dog progresses, the handler should be able to simply move over, instead of stepping in between the jumps.

7.   Send the dog over jump 1, command him to turn right and call him in between jumps 1 & 2. Command the dog to turn left, send him over jump 2, command him to turn right and call him in between jumps 2 & 3, turn the dog left and send him over jump 3, p.&p.

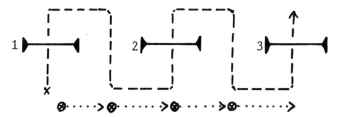

8.   Send the dog over jump 3, command him to turn left and call him in between jumps 3 & 2. Command the dog to turn right, send him over jump 2, command him to turn left and call him in between jumps 2 & 1, turn the dog right and send him over jump 1, p.&p.

9. Send the dog over jump 1, command him to turn right and call him back over jump 2, turn the dog left and send him over jump 2 again, command him to turn right and call him back over jump 3, p.&p.

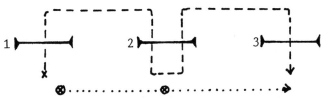

10. Send the dog over jump 3, command him to turn left and call him back over jump 2, turn the dog right and send him over jump 2 again, command him to turn left and call him back over jump 1, p.&p.

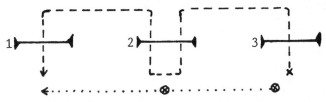

11. Leave the dog behind jump 1. Call him to you over jump 1, command him to turn to his left, send him over jump 2 and call him back again over jump 2, using the command for back jumping. Command the dog to turn to his left and send him over jump 3.

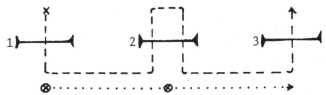

12. Leave the dog behind jump 3. Call him to you over jump 3, command the dog to turn to his right, send him over jump 2 and call him back again over jump 2. Command the dog to turn to his right and send him over jump 1, p.&p.

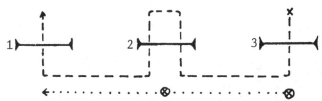

Don't let the dog get bored with this exercise — some dogs love it, others can only do a short session at a time.

Exercise 7

Aim of exercise - practise waiting at start, directional control and, teaching the dog to pay attention to the handler.

Equipment — 2 squares of jumps 6 paces apart.

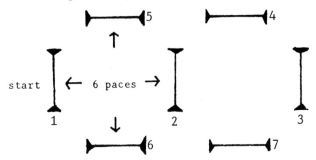

In the following exercises the dog is left at the start.
1.   The handler walks to stand behind jump 3 and calls the dog over 1, 2 & 3, p.&p.

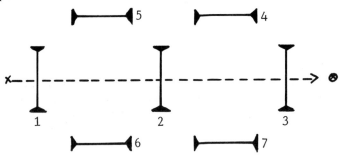

2.   With the dog to the left of the handler, leave him at the start. The handler goes and stands behind and slightly to the right of jump 2, calls the dog over 1 & 2, commands him to turn right and sends him over 7, p.&p.

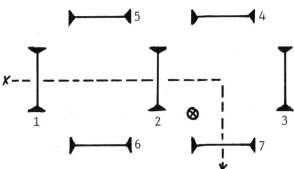

3. Repeat 2, but when the dog has jumped 7, command him to turn right. The handler moves to stand beside jump 6 and commands the dog to jump 6 (be careful to take the dog far enough back to jump 6 safely), p.&p.

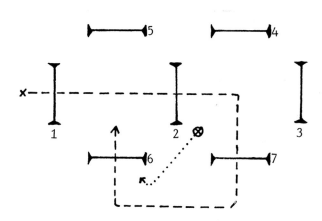

4. Repeat 1.
5. With the dog to the right of the handler, leave him at the start. The handler goes and stands behind and slightly to the left of jump 2, calls the dog over 1 & 2, commands him to turn left and sends him over 4, p.&p.

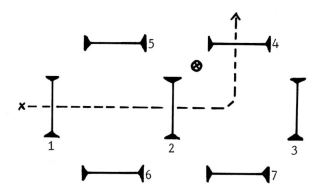

108

6. Repeat 5, but when the dog has jumped 4, command him to turn left. The handler moves to stand beside jump 5 and commands the dog to jump 5, p.&p.

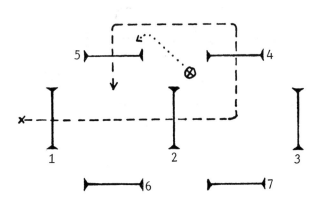

7. Repeat 3, but when the dog has jumped 6, handler and dog continue on towards jump 5 and the dog jumps 5, p.&p.

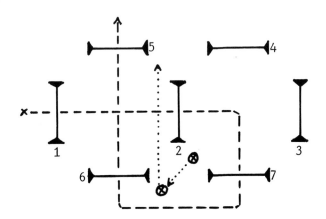

8.   Repeat 6, but when the dog has jumped 5, handler and dog continue on towards jump 6 and then the dog jumps 6, p.&p.

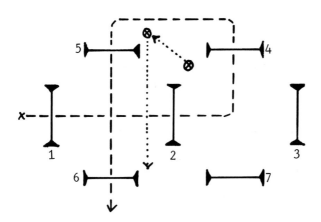

Whenever calling the dog to you over jumps, be careful that you give the command to jump at the right time. Many dogs are faster jumping towards their handlers, and late commands may cause them to mistime take offs, and so knock jumps down.

As the dog gets more confident at jumping, try leaving out the jump command, simply calling the dog. The dog then has to think out where to take off for himself.

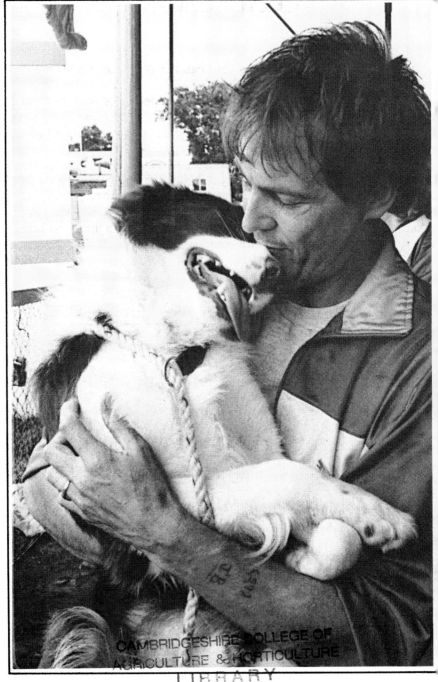

CONCLUSION

In this book I have tried to set the beginner off on the right course to enjoy agility with their dog.

Whatever you do, whether training or competing, always remember that a dog that is happy and enjoying himself, is much more likely to try hard to please you, than one that is afraid he is going to get told off for making a mistake.

Agility is a fast sport and more often than not, eliminations are caused by handler error. Don't be in a hurry to blame the dog. We ask a lot from our agility dogs and, although everyone wants to do a good round, I hate to see a dog being harshly told off for making a mistake. Working at top speed, it is easy for even an experienced dog to mistime a jump. Although we try hard to train a dog on the contact points, how do you explain to him that it is wrong to jump off the dog walk or scale in one place, when perhaps only 1″ lower it is fine?

Enjoy agility, make sure your dog does too, and learn to take the rough with the smooth. There's always another day and another show.